ILLUMINATING TRUTH

ILLUMINATING TRUTH

AUGUST RAINES

CONTENTS

Introduction	1
1 Historical and Cultural Perspectives	3
2 Literary and Artistic Representations	6
3 Scientific and Philosophical Interpretations	9
Conclusion	12
Enjoyed This Book? Let Others Know!	15

Copyright © 2025 by August Raines
All rights reserved. No part of this book may be reproduced in any manner whatsoever without written permission except in the case of brief quotations embodied in critical articles and reviews.
First Printing, 2025

Introduction

The concept of eternal light has captivated philosophers, sages, and visionaries across religions and artistic traditions for centuries. It has appeared as the solitary flame within ancient Hindu temples, the radiant companion of a singular savior depicted in European cathedrals, and as an aspirational ideal embraced by movements such as Jehovah's Witnesses, who promise the eternal light to those who follow the path of the Lord. Regardless of its form, this enduring light symbolizes humanity's collective yearning for transcendence and permanence amidst a transient existence. Even today, whether consciously acknowledged or not, this longing remains embedded in our cultural and spiritual consciousness.

However, the modern world, with its billions of inhabitants, seems increasingly detached from the infrastructure or even the conceptual embrace of eternal light. Thomas Edison, the father of the electric lightbulb and a self-described Deist, heralded artificial light as one of humankind's greatest achievements. Yet, this marvel has evolved into a tangled web of technological excess—one that sacrifices intimate, shared experiences of darkness to a relentless, industrial glow. The dominance of lamplight and its metaphorical association with power and control has been scrutinized by thinkers and writers, prompting a reexamination of how the metaphorical "light" shapes our relationship with darkness and intimacy.

In this evolving narrative of light and darkness, there remains potential for rediscovery—a revival of old ideas and traditions that may once again bloom. This reconsideration can be likened to the political allegory attributed to Bismarck, who reportedly told Count Helmuth von Moltke, the Younger, that "the seed corn in Dodendorf is as important as the essay in the editor's office." Here lies an opportunity not just to weigh and reflect upon our past but to plant the seeds of hope and meaning anew.

Background and Significance The image of an unquenchable universal flame serves as the heart of this collection. Eternal light is a concept that transcends time and cultural boundaries, touching disciplines as diverse as philosophy, theology, art, and science. For pre-modern Jews and Christians, particularly Byzantine Christians who drew inspiration from Jewish liturgical traditions, sacred nighttime vigils illuminated the eschatological liberation brought about by Christ's resurrection. The "eternal light" symbolized release from sin and death, offering a beacon of hope in the darkness.

In modern liturgical practices, these traditions endure. From the Christian East to the West, the eternal light remains a metaphor for "unfailing goodness" and contrasts sharply with the "darkness of sin and despair." For Tamil-Australasian Christians, emerging from darkened parishes with lights held high signifies the risen Christ breaking into creation—a moment steeped in symbolism and unity. Similarly, in diverse Muslim communities worldwide, pre-dawn adhān calls believers to rise together, facing eastward, to affirm their dependence on God. This daily act—shared shoulder-to-shoulder—demonstrates the unity of tawḥīd and devotion to the prophets' teachings, embodying a universal reverence for divine light.

The idea of eternal light unites cultures and faiths, reminding humanity of its shared dependency on something greater—a force that transcends human understanding yet remains deeply embedded in rituals, art, and life.

CHAPTER 1

Historical and Cultural Perspectives

The pursuit of understanding light as the unseen foundation of all existence has been a continuous journey—one that began in the spiritual and mythological traditions of humanity long before the advent of modern science. Across the globe, diverse civilizations and cultures have envisioned light not only as a physical phenomenon but as a profound symbol of harmony, intertwining the inner and outer dimensions of life. This integration of light into everyday existence gave rise to the belief in its eternal presence—offering enlightenment beyond the material world. The concept of eternal light, therefore, flourished as a governing theme in many cultural narratives, celebrated through grand ceremonies and festivals. While the scale and cultural expressions vary, the universal reverence for light as an eternal presence remains a unifying thread across humanity. This paper explores the cultural and religious perspectives that shape our understanding of light's eternal potential, interweaving its cosmological significance with the rhythms of everyday life.

Mentions of eternal light can be found across a vast array of cultures and histories. In ancient India, thousands of monks sought shelter in caves for yoga and meditation, where the roots of trees often penetrated through cracks, allowing light to find its way inside. This phenomenon, referred to as *Jyotirlingam*, symbolized the eternal light. To these yogis, existing in the darkness of ignorance, the wisdom of *Dharma*—knowledge and truth—became a radiant, ever-present guide. Ancient Vedic traditions preserved this reverence for light through the meticulously enunciated syllables of *Swaras*, which echoed light's manifestation through sacred mantras and chants, resonating through time as carriers of divine illumination.

Religious and Mythological Origins Eternal light has often been intertwined with religion and mythology, forming an enduring motif in the stories and rituals of both ancient and modern faiths. This symbolic light conveys a sense of the divine, representing hope, renewal, and spiritual awakening. Religious narratives have long celebrated eternal light as an emblem of transcendence. Joseph Campbell's concept of "the hero's journey" describes this shared mythology across cultures—where eternal light emerges as the rekindling of something infinite within the mortal soul, a guide out of darkness into divine connection. This universal metaphor underscores light's archetypal presence in human imagination.

Many religions also portray eternal light as a flicker of divinity within the human heart. In Christianity, this imagery expresses both the ideal and the suffering inherent in the human condition. God's eternal light, while infinite, bears witness to the trials of life on Earth. The Sufi poet Rumi describes this duality as "the opened center"—a state of clarity illuminated by life's constant ebbs and flows. Similarly, Buddhist traditions balance unity and variability, representing the Buddha and bodhisattvas as embodiments of the Infinite that remain immediate and tangible within the mystical dimension of life.

Mystical traditions across faiths often explore light as a direct, divine force. The Islamic philosopher Henry Corbin described "the Prophet of the Light" as a profound symbol of faith's hermeneutical depth. Ancient Babylon also held eternal light sacred, using richly illuminated sacred dwellings to honor household deities such as Homorocos. This guardian of the home symbolized law, structure, and refuge, with his flames perpetually burning to create a sanctuary amidst life's chaos.

The Aztecs, too, revered eternal light, lighting the first eternal flame at the Templo Mayor in 1325. Central to their religion was the belief that their gods required nourishment—sacrifices that mirrored the dualistic forces of nature and humanity. Each morning, the eternal flame was rekindled with the rising sun, accompanied by rituals like the Morning Star ceremony and offerings of fresh flowers. In ancient Greece, the idea of an eternal "sun" emerged as a metaphor for life, light, and omniscience, reflecting a timeless quest to grasp the profound and ineffable significance of light.

CHAPTER 2

Literary and Artistic Representations

At the heart of Deuteronomy's eschatological vision of light lies its prophetic depiction of the inextinguishable Temple lamp. This enduring symbol encapsulates humanity's hope for the ultimate triumph of light over darkness. The Temple lamp has left an indelible mark on art and literature, from its appearances on Pre-Christian sarcophagi to its intricate representations in medieval Winchesters.

One of the oldest surviving depictions of a menorah can be found in a mosaic at a synagogue in Ein Gedi, Israel, dated to 570 CE. Built into the shallow bedrock, this masterpiece endured the devastating earthquakes of the sixth century, remaining concealed beneath the ruins of the synagogue's upper floors until its rediscovery in 1971–1973. The mosaic's remarkable craftsmanship features a particularly large menorah, its arms gently spiraling inward, flanked by a *shofar* (musical horn) and an *etrog* (citron)—both symbols that hold enduring significance in Jewish prayer. Each of the menorah's seven branches is composed of vines adorned with ripe pomegranates and pairs of leaves, representing abundance and life. Although several parts of the imagery survive, scholars continue to debate the precise arrangement of its original twenty-one pomegranates, hinting at the depths of its symbolic meaning.

At Chartres Cathedral in France, the clerestory windows on the south side of the nave portray a breathtaking series of three lancet windows known as the "Tree of Jesse." These windows depict Isaiah's prophecy in 11:1: "A shoot shall come out from the stock of Jesse, and a branch shall grow out of his roots." The tree's vine-like structure, adorned with leaves and fruit, begins with a reclining Jesse at its base, releasing a lineage of men culminating in the Virgin Mary and the Christ Child. This tableau is enveloped in a forest of light and shadow, suggesting not the finality of the Last Judgment but the possibility of renewal—a new beginning where eternal light triumphs over a darkening world.

Key Works and Themes The theme of eternal light has inspired countless works of art and literature, exploring concepts like idealization, timelessness, hope, and religiosity. Here are some notable examples:

- **Paintings**:
    - Johannes Vermeer's *The Girl with a Wine Glass* (1659) captures an intimate, radiant light in its timeless composition.
    - Vincent van Gogh's depictions of snow-lit landscapes, including *The Parsonage Garden at Nuenen in the Snow* (1885), *Houses in the Achterstraat Alkmaar in the Snow* (1887), and *The Vicarage at Nuenen* (1885), embrace light's quiet yet enduring presence.
    - Johan Christian Dahl's moonlit landscapes, such as *View of Dresden by Moonlight* (1839–1841) and *Moonlit Landscape with a View of the New Amstel River* (1839–1840), celebrate light's transformative qualities.

- Samuel Palmer's works, like *The Willow* (1828) and *New Moon, a Riverscape* (1827), evoke mystical reverence through their interplay of light and shadow.
- **Literature**: In the Hellenistic period, Greek epigrams often described a world untouched by night. Parmeniskos's *Ekphrasis of the Island Thule*, preserved in the *Greek Anthology*, is among the most renowned examples, later translated into Latin by Catullus. Manilius, in his didactic poem, also reflects on the separation of day and night. Across antiquity, through the medieval and Renaissance periods, into the Baroque and Enlightenment eras, literature frequently referred to a lost paradise—an imagined realm of plenitude and eternal light. These depictions appeared prominently in apocalyptic and millenarian writings, often symbolizing the eternal hope of renewal.

Beyond the Greco-Roman golden age and the Edenic traditions of Christianity, other cultural narratives further enriched this theme. Utopian accounts written post-Age of Discovery, particularly those inspired by Ancient India, also envisioned the "sunny side of the planet" as an eternal sanctuary of light. Such richly associative imagery continues to thrive in mythology, folklore, and fairy tales, affirming eternal light's enduring role as a symbol of hope and transcendence.

CHAPTER 3

Scientific and Philosophical Interpretations

Throughout history, scientific and philosophical inquiry has sought to understand and explore the phenomenon of eternal light, conceptualizing it as the foundation of existence itself. While scientists strive to uncover empirical truths, metaphysicians and poets have celebrated eternal light as a manifestation of an intrinsic state—a luminous quality that can be rediscovered within oneself or perceived in the external world. For thinkers like Nikos Gatsos and Nikos Kazantzakis, eternal light resides in the materiality of existence, transcending the boundaries of the physical and the metaphysical.

The ancient Upanishads draw profound connections between the *Jyotishamatma* (luminous self) and celestial light, comparing the moon's luminosity to the radiance it receives from the sun. Eternal light is further expressed through concepts like *Jyotisham Murti* or *Jyotishmoorti*—interpreted as the embodiment of divine luminosity and the obliteration of ignorance. These interpretations emphasize the divine vision (*prakrit parv*) and spiritual enlightenment (*Purush Prajvalit*), portraying eternal light as a manifestation of unique and unparalleled divinity (*Purush apratima abhivyakti*). This involutive light not only dispels ignorance but also fosters knowledge, consciousness, and self-realization.

Scientific Explorations Scientists across disciplines—mathematics, physics, astronomy, cosmology, and cosmogony—have explored the principles underpinning eternal light. Theories of relativity, quantum mechanics, and cosmology have all contributed to this pursuit. In Quantum Physics, light is understood as the fastest medium, capable of traversing vast distances across the cosmos. Eternal light, in this sense, is conceptualized as a steady velocity or constant medium—*Stambh* (stagnant) and *Vel* (motion)—symbolizing both stillness and movement in the fabric of space-time. This scientific framework positions light as a fundamental mechanism for perceiving both visible and imaginary distances, reflecting its dual role as both reality and metaphor.

Quantum Physics and Metaphysics The elusive nature of eternal light transcends scientific definitions, appearing as a radiant force that bridges existence and infinity. In quantum terms, eternal light is perceived as an indelible, universal radiance, embodying an unbroken sequence of creation—a force that persists beyond the finite boundaries of time. This notion aligns with the concept of the "block universe," where the past, present, and future coexist as a continuous reality, illuminating the eternal nature of light.

Metaphysically, eternal light extends beyond empirical inquiry, inviting interdisciplinary, interfaith, and international perspectives. It serves as a unifying theme, connecting diverse forms of intelligence while retaining its ineffable nature. Rather than succumbing to mystical abstraction, metaphysics integrates naturalistic inquiry with transcendent principles. It seeks to establish systematic connections between diverse realms of understanding, enriching them implicitly without dismissing their unique frameworks.

By focusing on eternal light, metaphysics contributes to the dialogue between systemic change and informational theory. It provides a speculative lens that does not conflict with scientific or religious interpretations but instead leans toward the exploration of the unknown. This analytical perspective illuminates the profound and interconnected nature of eternal light, offering both a speculative and productive foundation for the future growth of knowledge.

Conclusion

As we examine the present exploration of the concept of eternal light within a darkening world, a pivotal question emerges: is there a singular eternal light, or do multiple eternal lights coexist within the diverse faith traditions we have considered? To address this, we must balance two critical perspectives. First, we must analyze the points of identification unique to each faith tradition, appreciating the distinct ways in which eternal light is perceived and integrated. Second, and equally vital, lies the opportunity to delve deeper into how individuals interact with these symbolic representations within their respective traditions. Such an inquiry fosters the potential for developing a nuanced understanding of eternal light as both a shared universal ideal and a reflection of diverse spiritual experiences.

For societies invested in nurturing social cohesion and strengthening global relationships, these questions take on profound significance. Exploring eternal light offers a rare and powerful lens through which we can identify commonalities across diverse beliefs. This work is not just a scholarly exercise—it is an essential contribution to cultivating dialogue and understanding in an increasingly interconnected yet ideologically fragmented world.

The implications of such an inquiry are far-reaching. It speaks directly to those who fear losing the foundational aspects of their identity, offering a framework for mutual understanding and respect. At the same time, it raises crucial questions about why individuals might distance themselves from engaging with another's concept of eternal light—whether it be divine, spiritual, or even atheistic in nature. These emancipatory undertones underscore the transformative potential of this inquiry, offering an entry point for future research into how concepts of eternal light can foster empathy, coexistence, and shared meaning.

Implications and Future Directions The findings of this exploration could reverberate across a multitude of disciplines, inspiring both theoretical and practical advancements. Here are several potential applications and avenues for future research:

1. **Transdisciplinary Integration**:
    - This work could catalyze the development of convergent paradigms, such as those bridging arts and sciences or cultural neuroscience and creative communication.
    - Opportunities abound for art-science collaborations, exploring intersections like neuroaesthetics and interdisciplinary storytelling frameworks.
2. **Psychological and Sociological Constructs**:
    - Future studies could delve into how the concept of eternal light might inspire new psychological theories or therapeutic approaches, particularly in contexts of psychosis and affective disorders.
    - Analyzing the role of eternal light in shaping individual and collective identity could offer insights into social cohesion and resilience.
3. **Architectural and Urban Design**:
    - Eternal light could inspire innovative architectural and urban planning concepts, creating environments that blend aesthetic beauty with symbolic resonance.
4. **Exploration of Zeitgeist and Aesthetics**:
    - Investigating the prevailing psychological and cultural aesthetics surrounding eternal light in our era could yield profound insights into contemporary human desires and anxieties.
5. **Political, Historical, and Cultural Dimensions**:

- The yearning for eternal light could be explored through the lens of political ideologies, historical narratives, and cultural movements, unveiling its broader societal implications.
6. **Fiction and Creative Narratives**:
    - Finally, the concept of eternal light could serve as a fertile launching pad for creative endeavors, from fiction writing to multimedia storytelling that captures its profound and enduring allure.

Equally significant are the more existential questions eternal light evokes, such as its connection to life, death, and the psychological desire to escape despair. These inquiries may guide the creation of deeply personal yet universally resonant narratives, expanding our understanding of this timeless concept.

Enjoyed This Book? Let Others Know!

If this book has blessed, encouraged, or challenged you in any way, I'd love to hear about it! Your review not only helps others discover this message but also encourages me to keep writing.

Would you take a moment to share your thoughts? A few sentences on what stood out to you can make a big difference.

You can leave a review on Amazon, Goodreads, or wherever you purchased this book. Thank you for being part of this journey!

www.ingramcontent.com/pod-product-compliance
Lightning Source LLC
LaVergne TN
LVHW092103060526
838201LV00047B/1558